UPSTATE MADONNA

LYN LIFSHIN POEMS~ 1970~1974

The Crossing Press, Trumansburg, N.Y. 14886

ACKNOWLEDGMENTS:

Magazines: *Ark River Review, Best Friends, California Quarterly, December, Diana's Bimonthly, Falcon, Granite, Greenfield Review, Hanging Loose, Hearse, Intrepid, Kasaba, The Little Magazine, Mississippi Review, New Salt Creek Reader, The News and the Weather, North Stone Review, Ohio Review, Poetry Now, Poetry Review: England, Rapport, Skywriting, Stooge, Unmuzzled Ox, West End, Wormwood Review.*

Anthology: *Mountain Moving Day, The Crossing Press, 1973.*

This project is supported by a grant from the National Endowment for the Arts in Washington, D.C., a Federal agency.

Cover & Title Page Design by David Sykes
Illustrations by Raymond Larrett

THE CROSSING PRESS SERIES OF SELECTED POETS

Library of Congress Cataloging in Publication Data

Lifshin, Lyn.
   Upstate Madonna : poems, 1970-1974.

   Bibliography: p.
   I.   Title.
PS3562.I4537U6   811'.5'4   75-11946
ISBN 0-912278-58-7
ISBN 0-912278-62-5 lim. ed.
ISBN 0-912278-59-5 pbk.

CONTENTS

DRIVING HOME

BIOGRAPHY

MEN ANYTHING SHE CAN PULL AROUND HER SHAWLS SHE

keeps things between her
self and other people
hair   the blank
words of a page
she says she sleeps
with everyone so
you won't know

wraps those words
around her like some
one else's mink and slits
the phone   when she
was young she squeezed in

to tight rubber girdles
waited behind a science
contest study of the
eye   now the
glass in front of her
eyes goes deeper
in than you can see

when she reads   or at
a party she dissolves
inside clothes that
can fool you for
days   she doesn't

believe in the stars
but her sign is the
crab and her house is
on her shoulders
most of what she sees

is like someone looking
out of some place
underwater where light
is something that twists
thru dark layers like
something you half
remember waking up

THOUGHT OF FACES ON

the walls of chartres,
of what lasts thru
war and fire. stone
dragged from as far
as bayonne, men
harnessed their
flesh to carts even
noblemen pulled with
their bodies. old
men whole villages
brought oil corn and
wine to those who
worked in silence.

i thought of staying
at an inn on the way
from our window the
church graves a
whole town from the
middle ages. blue
painted weathervane

picked up the
book and read "all
hearts were united"
they thought the
earth the whole
universe could be
interpreted by
measurable harmony

glass roselight
harmony bells

But my eyes drift
from the paper
to the last leaves
catching in mouths
of other trees,
saturday 2 hours
before amchitka

SOME UNBORN YOU

the one who isnt
you or might have
been   like a twin
who dies in a city
you cant remember
you almost see him
in mirrors   its his
dreams of lust his
anger you've told
to go away.   some
thing always with
you the more its
gone like the dead
soldiers dragging
those flags   their
coffins the woman
spun out of a car
onto the hood of
another like some
caught deer.   the
stain where her
heart was the red
spreading thru yr
sleep   something
off stage a foot
behind your own
unborn waiting
for yr shoes

I'LL SAY MONET THE NEXT TIME

1
what's incomplete
at the moment of

the accidental

there are no hard
lines in nature

i'll say monet the
next time someone
writes: but the

poems those
fragments   why
not make a long
poem slowly

you spread your
self too thin,
drawn to things
that can't stay

2
to see properly
is the hardest thing

he did the same
scene over and over

to see properly
the way what
ever moves
has a this-ness

you can touch

3
feel of stone
eaten by sun

something   just
at the point of
becoming   light
on the water

making the water
most itself

as it becomes
something different

FAT

some of it i've
given away, i guess that
comes from thinking
nobody could
want it
Fat. something you
take in and just
can't use
it hangs around
reminding you of what
wasn't totally
digested   a layer of heavy
water, grease

having so
much i'd dream the
4:30 tall thin
shadow thighs were
me, pressed so hard it
hurt   a
punishment   squeezing
myself into
me, into
what i didn't
want. afternoons
with the shades drawn
examining and hating what
i saw   longing for one of those
svelte bodies

i put the
scales back   would have
beat myself with
rubber chains

when i was 12 i bought a
rubber girdle   nobody
knew i peeled it off with the
door locked

somebody once said
you'll never get
cold this winter
fat legs
like that

how could something like fat ever
protect you from anything
outside   being only an
extension of yourself   cells
spreading   making you
more vulnerable
Fat people having more
places to bruise
or scar

i sat in a room and
watched the
river when
other girls
were going across the
state line,
were necking in cars at
lake bomoseen

despising those
layers i
didn't need

belly that
i hated and squeezed into
clothes a size
too small   hips but
worse   thighs i
hated them the
most   spreading out
on benches

once i lay on my
back cycling air until
the room spun

white waves of the body
i was so ashamed i wouldn't go
to the beach

my mother always
said   yes you're pretty
eat and i curled
into myself
eating what made
me worse

tho i wanted to
wear pleats
and be delicate

in one store a
man asked her
is it difficult
having one daughter
who's so
lovely and i
hated my sister for being
blond   her body

like a keen
waif   jealous of
her eggnogs and
chocolate
how meat had to be
coaxed to her
bones

you can't
camouflage   hold
anything in that
long   it explodes
a rubber girdle pops
elastic
letting go
then they know
that there's more
than you can
handle

look at me now and
you say   but those
thin wrists

listen   when i weigh
over a hundred i
break out in
hives   we

all think of our
selves the way
we were

especially when it
comes to what we
don't love

once when i was
walking home from
school the elastic
on my underpants died
The next day someone
wrote kike on the
blackboard
both i knew a result
of fat

i've never been good
at getting rid of
what i can't use
but that's when i
knew that i had to

that round face with
glasses   bulging
thighs   you know

when some man says
love it's still
hard to believe

If i wear my clothes
too short   it's to
remind   (look i
still avoid mirrors
glass) me that my

legs are not
unloveable   i

want you to see i finally am
someone you might
want to dance with

this me waiting under
neath on the
sidelines

years of
getting down to

It really is
sweetest close
to the bone

HAIR

in brooklyn one
love's aunt plotted
made an appointment
to have it done
cut in a flip

a present for me
like the scratchy
nylon gowns i
never wore when i
left to marry

an uncle said before
he died he wished
he could see it
short   after

the wedding i
pulled pins out of
that stiff hive
for a week   afraid
to touch it

when i taught in
highschool i had
to wear it up
sprayed it one
grey morning
with flit   as

if it was a
living flying
thing that
shouldn't   like
my life seemed
that october

unreal   i was
afraid to touch
it   all his family
tried to pull it
back into velvet

twist it   pin
it choke   they said
they wanted to see
my eyes but i
know they suspected
me of being a
hippie a witch

the college that
said i couldn't stay
on white cold paper
wrote first can't you look more
professional and

dignified   wear
it up   the brother
in law would pull
it sneer ask if i'd
seen the mad

haired girl in
the munsters   i
heard that the
whole tv season
later i learned that

what grew out of
the dark where i
couldn't reach
like dreams or
poems was beautiful

shouldn't be
squeezed into
changed into
something different

but those years
apologizing   stuffing
that sun bleached red
under my collar

straightening it in
what was ok for the
early sixties and
never letting it
go where it wanted

milkweed   wild
flowers   poems
animals a dream

hair like someone
who couldn't hadn't
wouldn't admit didn't
know it had a
life of its own

BLUE WATER

once it gets
in once you
let it stay

i close the window but
blue beats so
loud   it's
like living
with a man
you hate

it sounds
like the
roof could
fall   i can't
tell what good
can come of it

tho poems grow
like mushrooms
all night

WHAT YOU WANT: THE GARDEN GAME

i've been trying but
you slide away like
greasy stone   it
makes me feel i want
to pinch you bite

your neck till
you bleed   or are
you   i mean in yr
garden you wanted
mostly stone   stone

paths   stone that
pulls itself into
strange shapes
stone in all sizes
stone that reflects

the moon for you
the green is way
up   something you
may get to after
all this stone

you want a woman
without walls   you
say tho you don't
know it   stone
that slides around

you in the rain
is weathered smooth
as wood that
never intrudes

LEAVING MEN IN THE MIDWEST.
OR, SHE DREAMS SHE SLIPS

away like magic marker
ink in the rain before
its too late   before
she stays in cities
like madison or
oshkosh—watch
out in minneapolis
in green bay

Stoned on the lips of
men with strange
verbs with nouns
like dude and alkie,

dreaming from a bridge
a poet could jump
from   16 arms around her
brandy by dawn   If i

stay 2 more days
i stay she

whispers to the moon
licking the inside
of her damp thighs
floating   belly

eaten by
stars over the
fox river south
Under her the
ice shoves cold
ink in those
men's throats

Winnebago   menona
warming her nipples
Listen women like
this eat men and
spit the pits out
to make their
own dreams

(she used to dream
skin as the first
and last poem)

Now the magic marker
blond men dissolve   yellow
cornfields   they
lie down in
swallow them
They melt like
snow women.
Now this one is
making them into
poems that are flesh.

MOST OF THE DREAM I DON'T REMEMBER

except how his arm
held me like a comma
again   sliding down a

wet street   past telephone
booths full of desperate
people   his smile wider

than i'd remembered
long thin square fingers
i forgot to worry how

i'd fit him back in
my life   this time his
jacket wasn't full

of leaves   it was
strange not even
thinking of him for

so and then having him
in the room with mirrored
closets   where each

of us had been didn't
seem to matter   only his
shoes seemed new   dark

oxblood   there were
however problems   when
i unzipped him and

put my mouth down
close there was a nail
in his penis   and of

course really he
was dead   dead in good
clothes with a steel

box of bonds crisp
bills   mostly from rich
russian ladies

THE DREAM OF THE LETTER I'M WRITING YOU

of people moaning
repossess and the
mirror i walk into
trying to leave my
clothes on the other side

You once said it was my
unnatural wanting
to put everything in my
mouth to taste that
cut you off

I became what you
called me   haunted by
birds deep in the hills of
blood trying to
sing and biting wood

If you could see me
now   running in back of
glass   a man with an
accent touching my
skin lightly,

i wanted you
to come but you
said my
glass stopped you.
Feathers in the wind

leaves blowing
like in a movie just before
something big happens.
I used to dream you
might plunge your hand

into my heart
and soothe the bird's throat.
It wasn't till he
called me love that i
understood the truth

of mirrors. He
touched the parts that
he could most
easily first   then
deeper. Can you

handle where this
dream could go

STONE SOUP LEAVES

in the second
letter he said he
lived near water in
a house with no
sky except for the

light my letters
brought him   he wrote
of jails   the times
he threw stones all
day and wouldn't
talk   he said my

letters were the only thing
that touched him   my
verbs on his skin

it snowed all
april   i stopped
the mail 11 days then
wrote back   yes only
what if i'm not a
what if there's
snow between my

legs he said he
dreamed my nipples

i didn't think i could
hold him except on
a page he sounded
wild like a dream
i just could
touch waking up

the way i made his
paper face into
skin   love like a
city carved of
ice you know
about that one

chateau y kempe in
the mail that noon
i drank it in the
sun on the rug

dreamed incredible
positions but not
that he'd really

come   poems in his
broken shoes   lies
taped around them   i

drank cognac   shaved
my legs up to where
but i couldn't
find a drawer where
i could hide him

kept him like a special
delivery letter i'd take
and read in the tub

he was enormous   i had
to fold him in half
to keep him under the
floor in a dust

of moths   old lemons
silver dollars in his
mouth so no one would
hear him coughing

afternoons with the
shades drawn like a
half life pulling
more than could fit
inside   listening
for someone in the
driveway   the crush
of stones   the

stones in him like
the ones he
threw stones
piling on top
of other stones

as july blurred
in a cloud of fog
and nutmeg   he

taught me what men
did in prison   put
his tongue where
no one had

i pretended to like
the poems i knew were
stolen   like i
pretended with his

but he wouldn't
let me write   wanted
to revise my head
days i made

dentist's appointments
to be alone

then he started
opening my mail
answering my
letters   getting

busted in the
a and p   he
laughed at the
magazines i
read   said only
plath and dickey

i kept expecting
to find him dead

blood on the branches
in the mailbox
when he wasn't there
by nine the room
started to blur

a clock banged under
my clothes until he
rattled the back
door   and we'd

take a bottle and
crash in the leaves

i started to come
with him inside me

i wanted to keep
dreaming that was
all   like animals
that do things on
the run i was

afraid   places i
touched on him
seemed sharper

i wanted to i thought
he was a tree the
dead branches could be
cut off from   i

wanted to make soup
out of the stone

he got jealous of what
ever i wrote down
even what was
full of him   i

wasn't a cook   the
dust from all the stones

rubbing together blew
across the lawn

children followed his
tracks back in it

dreamt a man who
smelled of leaves

library books
in the oak leaves

days getting like paper
erased so thin in
spots you could see
thru it to where

dust gets more like
snow you couldn't
lie down in   but

i can still see
where we had

THE NO MORE APOLOGIZING THE NO MORE LITTLE LAUGHING BLUES

apologizing for going to
school instead of having
a job that made money
or babies

pretending i took the bus
to an office   paper
clips in my ear
and never that i was
reading wyatt
writing my own dreams
in the dust under the

apologizing for my
hair   wild gypsy
hair that fell out of
any clip   the way the
life i started dreaming
of did   apologizing for
the cats

if someone said my skirt
was too short i explained
or said sorry   but never that
i finally loved my legs

years apologizing for not
having babies   laughing
when someone pulled
a baby gerber jar out
of a closet and held it in
front of my eyes like
a cross or a star

i should have thrown that
thru the glass   i didn't
need to explain the music   they
listened thought it was
noise   said denim was for

children   i laughed   the apologizing
i don't want no trouble laugh
over the years pretending to cook
pretending to like babying
my husband

the only place i said what i meant
was in poems   that green like
forbidden flowers until they
couldn't fit in the house
pulled me out a window
with them toward colorado

i apologized for being what
they thought a woman was by being
flattered when someone said
i wrote like a man and for

not being what they thought
a woman   for the cats and leaves
instead of booties   for the poems

when someone said how much
do i get paid i pretended
pretended pretended   i
couldnt stop trying to please

the A the star the good girl
on the forehead   the spanking
clean haunted half my head
but the poems had their own life

and my life followed where the poems
were growing   warm paper skin growing
finally in my real bed
until the room stopped spinning for
good the way it had when i dressed
up in suits and hairspray

pretending to be things i
wasn't: teacher   good girl   lady
wife   writing about cocks and
hair for years before i'd felt
was still making love just on
the sheets of paper

when the poems first came
out one woman said i
can't take this   another said
i don't know   this can't be the you
i know   so brutal   violent
which is the real

the man i was with moved to
the other side of the bed
it was worse than not having
babies his mother said they
always knew i was odd

my hair and the books i
brought to bed   they
said i never seemed like
one of them

my own family thought it was
ok but couldn't i write of things that
were pleasant   they wanted to know how
i got paid and why i didnt write for
the atlantic   i

still have trouble saying
no   wanting most you's to
like what i'm thinking
to want my hair

i put a no smoking sign up
on the door but twice i've
gotten out ashtrays

but i've stopped being grateful   to
be asked to read   to have a hard
cock inside me

it's still not easy to get off the
phone tell a young stoned poet
it's a bore to lie with the
phone in my ear like a
cold rock while he goes on
about the evils of money,
charging it to my phone

now when i hear myself laughing
the apologizing laugh i know what
swallowing those black seeds can
do   spit them out like tobacco
(something men could always
do)   nothing good grows from the
i'm sorry sorry   only those dark
branches that will get you from inside

I ALWAYS WAIT TILL I'M ALONE
WITH PAPER TO SAY

even when somebody asks me
what i think of some
poem   i never told my

father love or the man
i live with   or the
things i hate   except in

a poem   who'd feel turned
on when there's a smell
of shit and anger   some

one talking baby talk
won't turn me   i never
even told the man who

came to fix things that
his smoke stayed in
my hair and i couldn't

stand   this is a poem to
the people who think
i've been direct with

them   it's for the men
who thought my legs
opening said what i

wanted   for one who
turned me from a comma
into a period coiled

tighter   spending money
for revenge   some poems
i wanted to hide even

before   i knew they
were me   the strange
love in them as

surprising   strange as
his own leg   to some
man watching his son

play football feeling
the smooth skin where
the hair was and it's

the first time he
thinks what this means

WANTING TO GET RID OF THE GLASS THE PAPER OR, I WON'T SING THE HARD SUMMER CRAB SHELL BLUES ALWAYS

wanting to not need rings
around rings   walls that
you have to figure
how to get thru

even tho i'm born
in july i don't
want all these
shells   i'm

coming to you naked
i want to say
what i never

like someone sleeping
under an open window   letting
in the stars   cold water   moon

WHAT IT'S BEEN LIKE WITH HIM
OR, THE MAN WHO LEFT FOR FOUR MONTHS
COMES BACK IN THE NIGHT LIKE THE MOST
AWFUL DREAM

there's a madman
drinking bourbon
on the stairway
listening in on
the phone i go
to sleep in torn
flannel and two
pair of opaque
panty hose after
he calls to say
sleep naked i
put ice on the
floor pretend
not to hear him
cutting holes in
my closet scream
i made him what
he hates so he
wants to burn
the floor all
women poems i
can't sleep till
i hear him snore
have a lover
waiting down
state if i
could just say
listen if i
knew the mad
house number
or could pack
in the dark if
there wasn't so
much smoke and
all the stairs
weren't burning

THE DREAM OF RIGHT HERE, OF PLEASING

In this dream i'm in a class with a
man i've been wanting   i keep
forgetting to read the

assignment   get there late
young girls   so skinny   their
long hair   suddenly

a man and i are sitting on a
bed with someone else   i
know what will

happen   sun thru the rubber
plants   snow   we talk about the
3 of us doing something

mexican bed   beads near the glass
twisting the sun cranberry
pillows the color of

blood too   i'm already imagining
the poem that will grow out
of   thinking   my

hand slips thru his fly a flower
grows from my neck   the men
merge   their lips blur

which should i please first
why are we moving from the bed to
a large circle inside

another circle   who is this
person across from me are
we both saying what we

he touches the green that i
wear like a pendant as
if he wants that instead of what

and i try to remember the last
time i cared who
pleased me   when i just

held who i wanted
which seems natural as easy as
sun on the skin of an

avocado right here

MIDDLEBURY POEMS

1941

there were spiders
over the carriage
i don't remember
my mother weighed
120 had bad dreams
of war   she took
money her mother
sent for clothes
bought pots and
pans   somewhere
across town my
father was flirt
ing in the brown
derby while she
read about left
overs   whispered
on the round stone
bench   merle doesn't
have to live like
this   heard the
words echo as loud
behind her almost
as a gun exploding

1944

sometimes there was chocolate

in radio stories there
were always tunnels
with germans in them

even the children dreamed
what they'd do to
young girls

there were no fathers

geraldine and priscilla
lived in the house with
turrets   crouched with
me in the march grass
friends until august
we made houses in the
queen anne's lace in
the stones while my
parents talked with
their father a baptist
minister he said later
we'd be afraid if we
didn't turn christian
his house smelled of
the same thing houses
i've been pulled to
since have   oil and
varnish   the long
polished stairs   teak
the bannister he held
on to when he caught
us with matches   he
acted as if it had
something to do with
not belonging to his
parish   the warts on
his hands seemed as
big as small eggs

THE FIFTIES

i was only 14
he pulled me into
a hole in the
leaves   i'd changed
my clothes 3 hours
to be right

he was the only one
of the 12 boys in
hillel   i wanted
to touch him his
iranian skin

one night in the
hotel over where
the dance was   but
i wouldn't let him
unbutton   or

in the apartment
on main street
where we both
felt guilty   i
knew i shouldn't
have taken off my

shoes   he was the
first of them i
wanted but wouldn't
a blood sun falling
behind the episcopal
church   my mother
whispering   listen
a girl in a
small town

CAT CALLAHAN

being fat until
that spring   i still
felt fat on main st
in my town but

not when the science
fair went north
burlington for 3 days
i met the kind of

long haired boy i
hadn't   the photograph
with my eyes huge
how the cop downstairs

groaned when he screamed
in with that ford
relatives squirmed at
his name   by june i

unbuttoned my sweater
wriggling in a back
seat near champlain
al martino's oh my love

i've hungered for so
the pink check dress
wrinkling a long time
as things inside

unchained were saying
yes yes tho i didn't

the minister's daughter
looks at her nipple in
a compact mirror
from ben franklin's

under the altar of
the Episcopal church
steps out of her
panties whispering
elvis. horse

chestnut leaves
leaves blowing up the
apartment stairs the

man who used to
watch them plunges
over the falls   lies

still as cabbages
under musty sheets
is falling into the
movie going back
wards   sneaks

across the state
line to bomoseen
for beer and a quick

MIDDLEBURY POEMS

near middlebury river
flint   some jasper

where water ate the
blueclay a huge kettle

flowers and leaves
on one side   charred
stones   arrowheads

a bowl made of stone
not found in new england

men   iroquois travelling
close to water kneeled

near the rushes grinding
corn in that stone

travelling from michigan
maybe   listened to

the river   otters
making arrowheads
in the creek

◆

coming in june on
log canoes   rafts
braided leaves for

a shelter   the
door south.   listened
nights to the fire

brook the wind
the red maples,
wrapped in blankets

from sussex   the
owls   coons the
wolves screaming

did the wool smell
like home   wrapping
deeper in it   the

catamount wailing
like a man
in pain

◆

the mouth of the
west river so packed
with salmon   looked
as if a man could
walk from stone to
stone on their backs

◆

the first lot began
with a walnut tree
south side of a

black ash swamp   the
east   white pine
south   witch hazel

coming down otter
creek   ice   1773
the first log house

built close to
the river   built
in the icy wind

Who had time to
imagine war

♦

chinking walls with
mortar   stuffing
holes   the windows

with fur   nothing
fragile could be
brought here

glass would break
dropping over the
trail of roots

some dreams   the
past like smoke.
hole in the ceiling

for smoke as for the
souls of the dead
in some indian houses

◆

in middlebury
an ear of corn
for rent   a

black man clearing
the land cutting
thru bramble

up the battenkill
made a cave in
a huge tree

otter creek lapping
against the blue clay
oxen in the night
grass   september

he leans against
the wet bark   feels
the earth his

the northern lights
coming right
down to him

♦

after corn
wheat for
white bread
oats   bacon
may grass   flax

strawberries grew
wild   black
berries   blue
berries

wild grapes.
the root of
sweet flag
for candy

in september
pigs were turned
out into the
trees   the

paths deep
acorn   beech
nuts   barley

♦

woods thicker than
any in england
1794   2 2-story
buildings   2 taverns
in the commons
mud   the tough
stumps of pine
trees the men who
got drunk and had
to dig them up
saturdays where
i'm writing this

◆

one man slipping
thru reeds lands
at isle aux noix
in a green clump
of willows   ties
the boat to white
pine.   later indians
won't give it back
he'll fire   they'll
hit   it's buckshot
in the brain   his
head cut off
carried on a long
pole up st john's
river.   o willow
willow

◆

this time they came on
friday when the men were

in the field.   elbad andrews
dragged across the lake

they broke in while his wife
was making curds   ate all the

cheese   dried apples in the
windows, nuts.   men moving thru

the kitchen like a bad dream
the fresh bread in her hands

shaking.   shells, mouths the
last thing she remembers

◆

troops moving thru lake george,
trumpets scattering the water fowl

◆

families buried chests
soap   hid chairs in
a pit of hemlock

thousands of melons
bursting in the
sun   the british

rode thru   burned
the whole   every
building but one

farm   its green wood
like some tough dragon
in the hot smoke

♦

escaping the first
of may   8 in a boat
cutting thru willow
split on the land
were caught escaped
were caught again

4 indians with
knives and guns
brought them to
three rivers   a
month later the

prisoners cut thru
the wood again a
rope from blankets
a bloody ox to

eat   **across** the st
lawrence to the
river sorel in the
same clothes 90 days
the cloth loose
rotting as it would
have in a grave

◆

running   baby over her
shoulder in a double gown
heading toward rutland

pewter in the earth
buried under the floor   a

vision of the thatch
burning   she sits

down   clutches the
log weeping what
will what

◆

crawling up the
mossy ledge, mt
defiance   the one
way up guarded
by the moon. each
man stooped   the
smell of damp
earth pine   let
another man climb
up on him.   in
the distance a
cougar, smoke.   the
men sounded so much
like owls no one
was suspicious

◆

finally they came home
over the deep roots

dug for what they'd
buried   some never

found the spot the
father dying.   one

mirror pulled from
mud   its frame

rotting   but the
glass showed the

dazed eyes of a
woman who still

couldn't understand

♦

july   young
boys   feeling the
spray from the

river the falls
near marble mill

ate plums apples
beans   marble

clay in their
fingers caught
eels in frog
alley told

secrets in
the damp moss
dreamed of

the skin under
linsey woolsey

◆

dark even after
she got there
snow shoes hardly
marking the tough
crust   one fire
in the school   a
young woman   face
as young as the
girls in front
of her   drifting
wonders   about that
man   the way he
smiled near otter
creek   comes back
shivering   takes
the girls' hands
pulls them in a
circle dancing
till blood comes
back to their faces

◆

no doctors, surgeons
they used herbs set
bones strangely   one
woman walked thru night
woods   6 miles on snow
shoes   washed the blood
from the sheets   from
babies' faces   2000
babies shining in
her hands like fruit

◆

spring   otter
creek overflowing

sweeping down fences
rails   one man took
his son on a
raft   watching
trout thru holes

willows turning
yellow the first
feeling of sun

april 20   warm
water on their lips

the current   the
water eating them
their last taste

no one ever found
the boy's body

♦

quarry road

the forge guns
for the state
made here   machines
for cotton   grist
mills over the
falls where frost
couldn't eat them
middlebury manufacturing
co., cotton, wool

in the mills   marble
for tombstones   dry
goods   shoes   until
fire ate most of
these buildings

♦

all this hair from
one family hung
on the wall

wreathes of hair
blond hair pulled

from a baby   hair
like grave grass
twisted under glass,
all this cut from
the heads of

myricks   russells

100 years ago

♦

main st   past
frog alley past the
bridge at otter
creek   the

cannon   white
spire on the
hill. in the
first room

of the house
black marble
cool night air
john sheldon

stuffing these
rooms with
clocks and pianos
stumbling thru

wire, keys letters
piled in closets
rooms like a
museum even

then   listening
for ghosts   maybe
taking out the
old maps   nights

alone   the
snow ½ way up
these windows
and no woman

♦

daughters who died at 22

at chipman's funeral
a raft made by lashing
canoes and boards   the
corpse with mourners
friends walking along
the river   crying

on the way the
boat leaked   men
bailed out the water
with their shoes

fragments.   businesses
that failed   the lots
getting smaller

even the tough pine
roots dissolving

♦

PEOPLE & PLACES

BLACKBIRD

hoarding arsenic
he fed it to
enemies
disguised as
sweet camash
invited anybody he
didn't like to
eat at his table

poison in the soup
he boasted life
and death powers
30 or 40 vomited
then died

later he slaughtered
his wife   she
was so young and
beautiful
her licorice
hair   he said he
couldn't help
being jealous

then was
sorry and
starved himself
to death
first asking that
his corpse be
lashed to a
grey horse
and taken to a
ragged bluff

they were
buried together
the horse
screaming as
earth came down

later the omahas
chose this mound
as the place
to welcome
white men

LEAVING THEM, LETTING THE FARM SWALLOW

drove away   i
know i'll never go

back and wanted
to write it down

the webs   old
crosses, marys

horses against the
sun   painted on
enamel   on the walls

she said i don't see any
hope for the
world we just take
in poison

kneeling with
4 german shepherds
at one door the
daughter

singing how sweet it is

her white arms

dissolving in the
night grass

THE MAN WHO TURNS EVERYTHING TO SHIT

the insecure man is
afraid   dreams no
thing he does can
matter   leaves shit
in his pants like
someone else might

write a poem   shit
is what he sees
himself as   he
doesn't know what
matters   when he
was small he threw
stones at the glass

buried toys the
day after they
stopped making
him forget what
he was   he was
33 before he
had a woman
and then only
the ones attracted
to shit and who
could like
someone who liked

that so he buried
them near the toys
behind the house
where his mother
died wondering
why no woman wanted
to make another
baby of shit

even as a child he
had few friends
he couldn't give
much   maybe some
shit just

think if it was
warm or green or
sex in all the places
i've had to write
shit   even anger
fighting   imagine
love   something
more than he can

his parents gave him
jaguars   chevrolets
daimlers   he wouldn't
talk to a girl he
didn't want to screw
bought 800 dollar

cameras   slim bikes
he never used   now
the nikon rusts in
the leaves   there's
mould on the pedals
his woman throws

up trying to wash
the brown stain
from her dreams
it's easy for him
to say he's crazy

i think it's the
shit   huge
unused chunks of
what he's pulled
stuffed and sucked

on   the greedy
baby   he wants every
thing that isn't
his and turns it
to shit fast

once he's got it
he wants to
get rid of it

he rarely gets to
the toilet on time

nothing   not the hair
of other men's women
not the new job
the new house   booze
that lets him sneer
nothing's really

new except more
shit   it leaks
thru his light
grey pants   it's
all he's able to
get out and i
guess he knows it

THE WAY HE IS WITH WOMEN: OR,
IT'S ALWAYS SHOW AND TELL WITH HIM

if he does some
thing he wants every
one to see it   the

way he leaves stuff
in his pants   he'll
bring the girl with

4 black lovers home
he only wants some
one already taken

slobbers on my best
friend   sniffing her
pants   but he hates

his penis   wants a
woman who can make
it do what it cant

some pretty slut to
give up all cocks
for him   what he'd

really like is a
woman with long
black hair   her wet

slit open on his
fender like a
dead deer

BLUE STAINS ON THEIR HANDS

went into the pines
and lived to be
97   old man
Dragon and his
six sons

they coupled with their
sisters in the dark
stone hills,
Ripton

suddenly they were a
tribe spreading
like fireweed

took over the
rusted out trailers
behind the blacksmith's

mushrooms and
blueberries grew
thru tin cans

they came down from
the hills for
whiskey and
to marry

none of them
didnt get
in trouble

blue stains on
their hands,
smelling of
leather

they kept their own
dialect and the
songs of the
old man

they'll still
kill for
a woman

DEAD MOLE

like a flat stone
except for 4 pink
such strange soft
hands   flippers
nearly   and the
tail to one side
as if embarrassed
for not being in
the right place,
on its back in
the ditch   seeming
to say excuse me
like a stone that
was naked and human

PHOTOGRAPH

in a t shirt   neck
wrinkling   something
to the right pulls
him   pleases him   the
joy   peace nearly
sucked in thru his
eyes travels down
into his fingers
holding the baby's
head   like a rare
expensive egg

IN THE HOUSE OF THE DYING
NOTHING IS NAMED THAT DOESN'T EXIST

like the snow world
of eskimos   days become

as they go
along   july

becomes what it
is as it goes

her face goes
someplace different

like the finger
prints on the
mirror   the place
on the wall where

she couldn't
stand   cancel

the trip to europe
blot out the heart

with cobalt.   like
eskimo carvings

often thrown out as
soon as they're made

words   the weeks
ahead dissolve

she goes to sleep on
her side in a snow

of pills.   tomorrow a flash
light in the thickest fog

POEM FOUND LISTENING IN THE PARK
TO ONE OF THE PEOPLE IN IT

everything i say you
argue with me
god damn bastard
didn't you want to
come to the park
everything i say
is wrong i don't
care if i die
you don't know
the law   the tires
are lousy   son of a
bitch   i can't depend
on you for you can't
even pay the
rent besides i'm
smarter than you
are   jesus christ.
62 dollars to buy
a lousy   you
could lose your
life   tires like
those   everybody
i know works   lousy
lousy   sick in the
head   the tires
you're crazy   get
out   what's the
matter anyway
who's yelling
you ass hole   who

THE FIRST WEEK

for 30 years i couldn't paint
flowers   then   after the
stroke i looked
at them again

now it's
flowersflowers

flowers   he says

playing the piano as if he
had at least 3 hands

THEY SAID

she just talked
to him like he
was a person,
nobody else had

it gave him ideas
they said later
when he slipped
thru grass like

the wild deer
between the
birches   she

just talked to
him like a woman
would to anyone
she had it

coming they said
when he came   put
his arm around
her from behind
said if you scream

MISS HOLDEN

tall and thin
a beautiful crane

in dark blue or
black silky clothes

chalk on the sleeves
not easy but not
the kind who put

stones in yr belly
mornings with the wax

smell in our noses
cutting apples and pears
bananas on the desk

but what i remember
most was the
shelf like an

altar that had nothing
to do with any church

that we could
decorate   i brought

in a velvet tapestry
with birds   a blue
bowl   candles

now the velvet
birds are mine

her life a half inch
candle   i can't
imagine what she

remembers in the
small gabled
house with one

old cat   was it enough
that a school was
named after her

HOLDING ON

the longest tall thin
legs in ballet
long straight
brown hair
a man saw you

on the ferry took
yr name yr
scrubbed skin
yr red wood eyes
under yr brother's

baseball hat
you giggled
into the waves
sure he wasn't
real and when

he called left
school to do a
something in a
movie   he cropped
yr hair painted

yr eyes green
later we heard he
beat you   you
were on many
covers that year

other girls thought
you were the end
not knowing yr life was turning
flat as that paper

falling down in
the street at 19
he said you were
becoming an old lady
wouldn't let you

eat   but you
were in that cola
ad with that
smile and no one
who saw you

squeezed behind him
on the cycle
knew then you
were just
holding on

PAPER CLIPS INSTEAD OF FINGERS

when her sister climbed
out of the window that
night with a baby just
starting   she shook
in her twin bed
2 hours before going in
to tell her father

he didn't beat her
but took off for a
few years in california
with two wives then
came back and drank
in the john where the
tile was falling

pat's eyes grew huge
and browner   tits
twisting against the
blue wool as her
cousins got knocked
up or left ninth
grade to join

the army   her
father cursed her
sister's list of men
listened at pat's
door when
he could stand
she didn't want a child

when she still felt
like one but it was
hard living at home
at 13 she miscarried
let paper clips circle
her arms instead
of fingers   sucked

typing paper
married a man made
of paper   lives
in a house her
old man never
could   some

times she thinks
if she could just talk
to the sister no one's
seen 10 years she'd
understand the nights

she lies twisting the
sheets into what
could be a rope
near the window she
starts to open
then bangs shut

FAT THIGHS & 30 DOLLAR EYES
(for Bonnie)

black at the roots
trying to sing a
glad song   gin

and tonic afternoons
her daughter falls
in a pool of water

her son doesn't
understand the men
moaning in his
father's pillows

phones haunt her
if her husband would
only get deaf faster

Eye lashes glued on
top of her own for
thirty dollars

she opens fat thighs
to anyone and knows
that nothing anyone
can touch about her
is real

SUNDAY

we sleep right together
listen to leaves   he
says his fingers
get cold from
playing   slips
them in my hair

listening in the
sheets to "my
woman is water"

do all men who
play guitar

get such
beauty from wood

i wonder   slipping
my hand into where
he never wears underpants,

wanting to be
that warm

MONDAY 3:10 STICKY WINE GLASS ON THE RUG

went to sleep too
early hugging the
warm pad like
somebody's skin

the drugged black
like stars the
clouds blew over

fast now its
like feeling pain
thru demerol
thru codeine

TUESDAY

wanting something to
put my hands on touch

to hold like the smooth
dark chestnut my

grandmother held those
afternoons in the

room the ferns would
die in farther away

than she could see

WEDNESDAY

lying in the sun
using everything:
yr hard thighs
beret wind
blows the grass
like water i'm
writing this poem
about you when
you're suddenly
here picking wild
asparagus i
jump up sweaty,
lose the last line

startled/ guilty
it's as if i'd been
playing with myself

THURSDAY

last night's smoke
in my hair

smoke and bourbon
the first day

of november
it's dark

before 5   the

day   a leaf   a

moth with a
broken

wing twitching,
hitting glass

FRIDAY

i'm thinking of somebody's
poem about the lovers

how each one imagines
and go upstairs   the

room spinning   when
you come up you

ask if i want you
to go   even sick

love i want   and you
put your fingers

in my juice but i
black out dream

you run off with a
new girl's short

hair when i
thought i had you

SATURDAY

glazed rose branches
scraping frost with
a knife stained with
blueberries   blue
berry kiss   wearing
your blueberry shirt
high and light as
the rockets we send
up over the wood pile
as the ice cracks in
the pond and we move
back a little   kneel
in the snow where
deer have since noon

DRIVING HOME

NEW HAMPSHIRE

wild cat in the
wood pile   deer

you cant see
i drift with

the poem you
sent into an

underground
river where

indians eat
fish so old

they have no
eyes. if i

shut my eyes
i hear the

water that
flows under

the columbine
When i touch

the chair i hear
bluebirds that

were wild in its
leaves when there

were red flowers
in its branches

THE LIGHT

stretched out in
indian paintbrush
under very small
green apples   the
sun making my hair
red   i'm talking
to susan   one white
cat in the unmowed
grass   the light gets
nearer, i can taste
it on my fingers

ALL NIGHT BOOGIE

still going on
under the window

billy singing
tennessee blues   a

hill of ballet
slippers   jenny's
borrowed bed

feeling easy
waiting for you

waiting for rain,
for hail big as plums

BLUE SLEIGHS

December   the
water moves
dark between the
snow dunes in ten
thousand hills
pulling light
around the
black stones, a
sound to sleep
and love by
like bells
running thru the
children's sleep
when they dream
of blue sleighs

GOODBY   GOODBY

when he said he
was finally glad to get
rid of that piece
of shit   i asked
if he meant the
house   the car
or maybe me

DRIFTING

thinking of what the
poet said last
night about
bodies   how not
having control
over yours is
being a slave

still i can't
answer yr call.
orange leaves   it's
the end of october
again   a chestnut
on the sill from
versailles   i

remember my
father sitting
under a chestnut
tree that fall
in vermont   he

never said a
thing except
"never do what
you don't want"

which wasn't the
way it went for
him   snow

by december   he
drifted into that
deep cold before
he could change,
his broken face
locked in pine

WILDFLOWERS, SMOKE

1
baby i want to see yr
thing   is it   oh you're
so good to   do you
like my meat in yr mouth

2
sunday the green vines
catching the water. Leaning
against them   the
wet berries

i left before it got light.
All day you lie in the sun
near the falls washing the
night off (are all southern
men as suspicious of what
they can get)

later i wrote you from
rome knowing you have
no place in my life
except you're so symbolic

3
is that why the poems are
fragments are pieces   i've
been wanting them to
connect the way
i've been wanting my
life to. But it's
all milkweed

4
even the first night
you said we can't.
Tuesday, flutes and
bells   clarinets
rain on the slanted
roof   if i get up   do
anything too fast
in here   the way i
did with you (my hair
catching in yr lips)
everything starts spinning

5
yr small bones
choctaw indian
spider medallion
scraping our skin.
It's been hard for you
all night you
say does this
choke you

6
fingers like
yours always
let go. i need
a new black
cat bone. smoke
in the air   i've
been here before
blown by night

7
nothing in my
life grows out of
itself like
quartz

tho i've wanted to
write poems that
do   but they're

more like
wildflowers too
wind songs rooting
in abandoned places

barry is that why i
chose men like you
dark places   deserts
no settling down
safe gardens with
fences like rhyme

ANGER

tired of sucking it
inside like stones
that build from the
belly up to the tongue
trying to surface
grinding on each other
the dust smokes in yr
eyes   soon yr lips
will be frozen   the
weight pulling you
down in a snow you
can't move from unless
you spit the stones
out   let them break out
of you like a grenade
a flower

LIKE A CARBON INSIDE

the last few days i can't
wait to get away from you
and write even this down

it's strange   this lust
for an instant replay
double your money   love

i go over your blues the
laughing to keep from

you said   can't you tell
the way i touch you (blue
feathers   apples   rum,
your marks on my arms later)

it's as if there was a
carbon under my skin in
my blood pulling back
holding on to what there
is more than enough of

PHOTOGRAPHS

hands lightly
holding   caught
in the small
touching yr chest,
a strange jewel
and my face my
eyes enormous
the sad look
in yr eyes too

And we thought it
would turn out
a porno

A SMALL AT THE/ UNDER THE TABLE POEM

even in may there's
snow in the dark
places   In india
there's so much sun
rau says every one
is ten years older
I see us in an igloo
under the table   our
skin burning like oil

DREAM OF THE DREAD BIRD

a dread bird
sits in the
black walnut
he's been there
a lot lately
his beak splits
the moon   his
feathers on my
pillow   i can't
breathe   forget
my arms wrapped
tight to stop
his claws like
a woman who
just touches
her own breasts
feels for lumps

TOO EARLY   OR WALKING AROUND SAYING
NO THIS CAN'T THIS

cats fur in the darkwood corners
ashes blown under
the bed   for four
months we drove
by nights stoned
on the thought
of moving in   now
i have to remember
what the groan in
the furnace means
sleep on the left
side of the brown
bed   wake up dazed
i forget why i'm
alone   sun at 5
am on the dining
room table thru
ragged chestnut
branches   fills
the house with a
warm false light

JOY RIDE

for 8 months
following me like
· an incubus
loving me for
lies i make on
paper   he
tried to do
that and threw
them away the
way he did his
women   five
wives   the babies
clearing out his
houses the way
is it the eskimos
burn jackets
wine   letters
went too   paintings
But the holes
he tried to
stuff me into
one dreaming
maybe some
super joy
ride, grabbing
my life like
it was his
own long clitoris

AFTER THE NIGHT FLOWERING. OR,
WHEN THE SUN IS

i want to be like
a tree that sing-
ing things live
in until i learn
to sing too   but
i've picked men
stoned on dead
leaves   the wild
red of their dying
men who appear
like mushrooms
over night   a
leg pressed to
mine in the car,
mushroom breath.
some write letters
first, have eaten
a poem.   he did,
last night's pale
shadow   his hands
shrinking from sun
who is probably
revising me now
thru marijuana
in the tub   touch
ing stars in the
water   the only
things he'll touch

THERE WAS ALWAYS GREY

rain she says
and strawberry
wine in our
room over the
rag shop. you know
i gave the child
away then he
left went
back to africa
sells drugs down
the coast. every
thing gets clearer
the farther away
you get like
in a plane she
says but he was
so gentle his
hand in me,
loving me all the
way to dekalb

ANY NIGHT THIS TIME OF YEAR

That guy at the
bar with broken
shoes and moaning
about literature
and such, don't
pay attention
it's lies
and he knows it,
drunk as midnight
it's just he's
got it bad
for a girl with
fat thighs
who chews her
hands in her
sleep and
doesn't
want him

NOT THINKING IT WAS SO
WITH YELLOW FLOWERS

At night I
dreamed that
same dream,
the one
full of muscles
and thighs
that aren't you.
Later the fear
came back
crossing into
Mexico tho
at first
when I woke up
I thought it
wasn't true
the air was so
bright and
yellow flowers
were falling
from the
pepper tree
like suns

THE INTERVIEW GOES ON DREAM

in the warm grass after
the concert   the
smiles that are folded
in paper played
back   and yr hands,
they don't break
anything this time.
Torn strings grow
back together   and
the bird in the
branch just over us
shits horizontally

THE CHANGE, THE

not to be
to each
other any
thing   less even
than hill or
leaf   the
unwinding
          this
putting the
shells back
near the sea

LAYING OVER WAITING,
CANAL STREET   BUFFALO

waited here for
passage to the
west   waited
in taverns in
dance halls a
murder a day on
the buffalo water
front. laying
over got to
get on that
steamer west
boozing by 11   the
fights, singing
make rome by
7. damp wind   rum
red light on the
water.   500 ladies
of the evening
in silk every
night when
the sun goes.
o buffalo girls

: like the kind of
pine that can grow
where everything
else has been eaten
by fire   the seeds
safe in the dead
tree's closed cone

BIBLIOGRAPHY

BOOKS:

Why Is The House Dissolving? Open Skull Press, 1968.
Leaves and Night Things, Baby John Press, 1970.
Black Apples, New/Books (The Crossing Press), 1971.
Lady Lyn, Morgan Press, 1971.
Tentacles, Leaves, Pyramid Press, 1972.
Poems by Suramm and Lyn Lifshin, U. of Wisconsin
at Madison (Union Literary Committee), 1972.
Moving By Touch, Cotyledon Press, 1972.
Mercurochrome Sun Poems, Charas Press, 1972.
Black Apples (enlarged 2nd. ed.), The Crossing Press,
1973.
Museum, Conspiracy Press, 1973.
Poems, Konglomerati, 1974.
The Old House on the Croton, Shameless Hussy Press,
1974.
Forty Days, Apple Nights, Morgan Press, 1974.
Audley End Poems, Mag Press, 1974.
The Old House Poems, Capra Press, 1975.
Blue Fingers, Shelters Press, 1975.
Plymouth Women, Morgan Press, 1975.
Thru Blue Dust, New Mexico, Basilisk Press, 1975.
Shaker House Poems, Omphalos Press, 1975.
Poems, Conspiracy Press, 1975.

ANTHOLOGIES:

Mad Windows, Lit Press, 1969.
Remember Our Fire, Shameless Hussy Press, n.d.
New American & Canadian Poetry, Beacon Press, 1971.
From Feminism to Liberation, Schenkmann Press, 1971.
In Youth, Ballantine, 1972.
Modine Gunch Anthology, M. Gunch Press, Madison,
Wis., 1972.
Rising Tides, Washington Square Press, 1973.
Psyche: The Feminine Poetic Consciousness, Dell, 1973.
Mountain Moving Day, The Crossing Press, 1973.
I Hear My Sisters Saying, Thomas Crowell, forthcoming.
Pictures That Storm Inside My Head, Avon, forthcoming.